DAVY CROCKETT

Retold by Felicity Trotman
and Shirley Greenway
Illustrated by Chris Molan

Raintree Publishers
Milwaukee

First published in the United States of America 1986
by Raintree Publishers
310 West Wisconsin Avenue, Milwaukee, Wisconsin 53203
in association with Belitha Press Ltd, London

Conceived, designed and produced by Belitha Press Ltd.
31 Newington Green, London N16 9PU.

Printed in the United States of America.

3 4 5 6 7 8 9 10 11 12 13   99 98 97 96 95 94 93 92 91 90 89

Note: The story of Davy Crockett (1786-1836)
is a mixture of fact and legend—as it was in
his own lifetime. Our text and illustrations
have been based on many contemporary
sources, including the *Davy Crockett Almanacks*
(published in the 1830s), on his autobiography,
*The Life of David Crockett, the Original
Humorist and Irrepressible Backwoodsman*, and
on *David Crockett, the Man and the Legend* by
James Atkins Shackford.

F.T. and S.G.

Down a narrow track between thick strands of cottonwood and sycamore trees walked a man driving a herd of scrawny cattle. By his side walked a thirteen-year-old boy. His name was Davy Crockett and he was running away from home.

avy was a typical backwoods boy, perfectly at ease in the great wild woods near his home in the border state of Tennessee. But he had no time for book-learning. His father, John Crockett, was an unlucky man, and the more his troubles grew, the more uncertain became his temper. Davy faced an uncomfortable choice: he'd be beaten by his father if he didn't go to school and by the schoolmaster if he did! So he'd hired himself to Jesse Cheek, the drover, and was on his way to Virginia.

4

It was three years before he returned. Time and his many adventures had changed Davy so much that no one recognized him. But as the young stranger sat down to eat with the family, his elder sister looked closely at him and cried: "It's Davy! Here is my lost brother." The family was overjoyed and the hickory stick stayed firmly in its corner from then on.

To help pay some of his father's debts, Davy hired himself out to the neighboring farmers. But his experiences had made him wiser too, and he began to regret that, at sixteen, he had not yet learned the first letter of the alphabet.

At that time he worked for a kindly Quaker whose son kept a school. They agreed that Davy would have lessons on four days each week and would work for the schoolteacher on two more. In six months, the naturally quick-witted Davy had learned to read, write, and do simple arithmetic.

Davy also had another plan. By improving himself he hoped to gain a wife, and when he was eighteen, he was introduced to a pretty Irish girl called Polly. In spite of her mother's disapproval of the penniless young man, Polly agreed to marry Davy. The young couple was very poor and Davy soon realized that looking after a wife and small children was very different from hunting free in the wild woods. He began to grow restless.

It was at this time that the Creek Indians declared war on the white settlers who had taken their hunting lands. When Davy heard the news, he knew he must go and fight. Polly was horrified and begged him not to leave her.

"Polly," said Davy, "it's hard for me to leave, but if every man waited until his wife got willin' for him to go to war, why then, there'd be *no* fightin' done, and we might all be killed in our beds. I'm fit and strong and a good shot and I owe it to my country."

Polly said no more and Davy signed on for sixty days of service. The army was commanded by General Andrew Jackson. Davy soon became a scout and was sent into Creek territory to seek news of the war parties. He found a farmer named Radcliffe who was married to a Creek woman. Radcliffe told him that ten painted warriors had passed by only an hour before. Davy and his men followed.

Before long, they camped for the night. Suddenly Davy was awakened by the "sharpest scream that ever escaped the throat of human creature." It was the war cry of a Creek scout. Davy learned that the Creeks had been crossing the Coosa River all through the day and meant to attack Jackson.

This news sent Davy rushing headlong through the moonlit night to warn the army. He covered sixty-five miles in just ten hours, yet found, to his fury, that nobody believed him. When an officer arrived several hours later with the same story, everyone was ordered into action.

When Davy and his friends had served ninety days, they decided to go home. They were tired, ragged, and hungry, but General Jackson said no one could leave. Davy Crockett's motto was: "Make sure you're right, then go ahead."

He knew he was right this time. He led the volunteers past the armed soldiers, and even past the angry General himself. They never looked back and he led them all safely home.

D avy went again to the Creek Wars and fought well in many battles. He was so skillful that he always came home safely. However, his patient Polly was not so lucky. She died after their little daughter was born and Davy sadly tried to look after his family alone.

Then he met a woman called Elizabeth whose husband, too, had died during the Creek Wars. She had small children to look after, and so she and Davy decided to marry and bring up their large family together.

On their wedding day, Davy and his guests were waiting for his bride to arrive. Suddenly a pig hurtled through the door, grunting loudly. Everyone laughed heartily. Davy strode up to the pig and turned it out, saying solemnly: "Old hook, from now on *I'll* do the gruntin' round here."

Indeed, Davy Crockett was already as famous for his humor as he was for his skill as a hunter and woodsman. Once Elizabeth was told that her husband had died in the forest. When he arrived home, safe and well, Davy declared, "Well, I know'd that was a whopper of a lie, as soon as I hear'd it!"

Davy moved his family to the far west of Tennessee. It was such a newly-settled part that it hadn't yet any ordinary government. Davy's fame as a woodsman and war hero, along with his humor and honest courage, made him popular with his neighbors. They asked him to help them to look after their new lands.

When official government came, at last, to western Tennessee, Davy became a magistrate. He had no training, but he said, "I gave my decisions on the principles of common justice and honesty between man and man, and relied on natural-born sense and not on law-learning to guide me."

Davy became a very important man in his home state. He was made a colonel in the local militia, an honor which delighted him, in spite of his distrust of generals. He was elected to the Tennessee State Legislature. Now he was one of the men who decided how he and his fellow settlers were governed.

However, like his father before him, Davy always failed in his schemes to make his fortune. He and Elizabeth built a mill which was swept away in a huge flood, leaving them homeless and deeply in debt.

"Always pay up when you have a bit's worth left in the world," said Davy. And so they sold their lands, paid up and moved on again to the untamed banks of the Obion River.

Out there on the frontier, the settlers had to store as much meat as they could to feed their families through the long winters. The best meat of all was bear. But it was also the most difficult and dangerous to get. "Will you hunt bear for us?" his neighbors asked Davy. There was nothing he liked better.

So on a cold January morning, Davy and his dog Teaser went out after a bear. He tracked it all day and by nightfall he was lost. His clothes were wet through and there was no dry wood for a fire. Davy knew that he must keep himself warm if he was to live through the icy winter night. He climbed to the top of a tall tree, and then slid quickly down again. This warmed him so much that he spent the whole night doing it over and over again! But during the rest of that winter Davy's family and friends had plenty of meat—for he reckoned he'd killed one hundred and five bears before the spring thaw.

Once again Davy had a scheme by which he hoped to make his fortune. He and his friends built two boats, loaded them with barrel staves, and set off down the broad river toward New Orleans. But the Mississippi was a treacherous river, and soon the landlubbers were in trouble. They could not bring the boats to shore, and so, lashing them together, they sailed on through the night.

Davy was in the little cabin, wishing he were hunting bear, when the boats hit a mass of driftwood. There was a crash and the two boats upended. Water poured down the hatch, trapping Davy in the cabin. He thrust his body through a hole in the wall and shouted for help. Wedged tight in the hole, Davy was about to go down with his boat, when his friends began to pull. They tugged and tugged until Davy popped through that hole—"literally skinned like a rabbit"—leaving all his clothes behind. Once again, Davy and his friends had lost everything and had to borrow money to get home.

16

In the spring of 1827, Colonel Crockett made a decision—he would run for Congress. He was no speechmaker but his listeners loved his funny stories and down-to-earth opinions. Sometimes, though, he had to buy them drinks to hold their attention. Davy never had much money, but on one occasion, he traded a fine raccoon skin for a round of drinks. Then, unnoticed by the barman—who had cheated his customers often—he picked up the skin and did the same trick again. That coonskin paid for ten rounds of drinks that day!

The voters felt he was one of them and Davy won
the election handsomely. He took his seat in the
House of Representatives and set about trying to help
the poor backwoods people of Tennessee. He wanted
to make sure that the people who worked on the land
could own the land. When Davy first came to Congress,
he supported the party of his old commander,
General Jackson, who was running for president. But
Jackson acted more and more like a politician and
less like an honest frontiersman. He lost Davy's
support.

The Whig party was also opposed to General Jackson. The Whigs invited Davy to visit them in the East. He went to Philadelphia, New York, and Boston and made friends wherever he went. As he traveled he made many speeches. The Whigs liked Davy's blunt and humorous way of talking. When he left Philadelphia, his hosts presented him with a magnificent rifle. Davy was delighted and named his new companion Betsey.

In 1835 there was another election. But the government was growing tired of this outspoken frontiersman who attracted so much attention. Back home the settlers, too, had had enough of waiting for Davy to get his Land Bill passed. When the voters were offered twenty-five dollars each to vote against him, few could resist. Davy lost the election but knew that he had always done his duty and spoken truthfully to the people of Tennessee.

Upset by his defeat, Davy grew restless again. He needed something new and exciting to do. When he heard about the trouble in Texas, Davy decided at once to offer his help. Texas was under Mexican rule, but many American settlers were attracted to this rich land. Soon trouble arose between the independent, freedom-loving Americans and the harsh government in faraway Mexico City. The Mexican leader, Santa Anna, led an army into Texas to crush the troublemakers.

The call went out to all the settlers to take up arms to defend themselves. The Texas militia, under Colonel William Travis, gathered to fight for their independence. Davy and his two companions headed for the town of San Antonio de Bexar, where the little band of soldiers had taken possession of an old fort—called the Alamo.

As they traveled downriver by steamboat, Davy met a tall, lanky "sea serpent-looking" fellow. This man, "Thimblerig" by name, took his fellow passengers' money with a gambling game played with three thimbles and a pea.

Davy took his turn at the game. Thimblerig moved the thimbles with his quick fingers, but Davy, with his knife in his hand, picked up the thimble of his choice. There was the pea. The two became friends and Davy convinced Thimblerig to come with him to Texas, saying: "If you cannot live like an honest man, then die like a brave one!"

When Davy and his companions arrived in Texas, they met a young man, a bee-hunter, who offered to guide them across the prairie to join the militia at the Alamo.

Colonel Travis was a young man, headstrong and stubborn. He had refused to recognize the authority of General Sam Houston, commander of all the military forces in Texas.

General Houston sent Colonel Jim Bowie, the famous fighter, with orders for Travis. He was to abandon and destroy the fort. But Travis declared that he would make a stand. Jim Bowie chose to remain and fight beside him.

Santa Anna soon surrounded the Alamo with his army of five thousand men, and began to bombard it with his cannon. Travis sent a desperate message out of the Alamo: "I shall never surrender or retreat. I call on you in the name of liberty to come to our aid with all dispatch . . . Victory or Death!"

Thirty-two men answered his call and found their way into the besieged fort. Travis now faced the full might of Santa Anna's army with just one hundred fifty men at his side—and Jim Bowie was already dying of fever.

For ten days the Mexicans battered the walls of the Alamo with their cannon. The little band of defenders fought back furiously, losing many of their number, but making the enemy pay even more dearly. Davy was such a good shot that he and Betsey could pick off the gunners before they could fire their cannon.

Then one day the bee-hunter was hit. Davy rushed to his side but found the man only stunned. Davy pulled a small Bible from the man's breast pocket—in its pages lodged a musket ball!

The defenders were brave and resourceful, but as the days passed they grew weary. There was little food and no time to rest. But still they fought on, losing their comrades but never their determination.

Before the dawn on Sunday, March 6th, 1836, Santa Anna attacked the crumbling fort with more than two thousand men. Travis cried: "The Mexicans are upon us. Give them a fight!"

The battle raged for five hours while the sun climbed high in the sky. When the Mexicans at last broke in they were astonished at the courage and ferocity of the few remaining defenders. Each man fought to the end, a pile of bodies ringing the spot where he stood. Travis went down, taking many with him. Jim Bowie leaned on his pillow, firing his pistols, until he, too, was overpowered.

Through the noise and smoke, the Mexicans saw Davy Crockett alone in an angle of the wall. He held his shattered Betsey in one hand and in the other swung a great hunting knife. His friend Thimblerig lay dead at his feet. Davy was killed where he stood, one of the last defenders of the Alamo. He was in his fiftieth year.

D avy Crockett was truly larger-than-life, and his adventures had made him a legend long before he died. Amazing tales were told of his skill and daring: he could hug a bear to death, bite the head off a rattlesnake, and whip his weight in wildcats. After the Alamo, the stories grew wilder and wilder, until the real Davy almost disappeared behind the legendary one.

But it was his own people who missed him most. The frontier people of Tennessee cried in the streets when they heard he was dead. Davy had been their champion when he lived and they remembered him in their own special way.

"There's a great rejoicin' among the bears of Kaintuck. The alligators of the Mississippi have grown so fat and lazy that they'll hardly move out of the way of a steamboat!
Rattlesnakes come out of their holes and frolic, and foxes go to sleep in the goose pens.
And all because the rifle of Crockett is silent forever.
And the print of his moccasins is found no more in our woods."